Massacre at Myall Creek

John Summons

CAMBRIDGE UNIVERSITY PRESS
Cambridge, New York, Melbourne, Madrid, Cape Town, Singapore, São Paulo, Delhi

Cambridge University Press
The Edinburgh Building, Cambridge CB2 8RU, UK

Published in the United States of America by Cambridge University Press, New York

www.cambridge.org
Information on this title: www.cambridge.org/9780521447638

© Cambridge University Press 1993

This publication is in copyright. Subject to statutory exception
and to the provisions of relevant collective licensing agreements,
no reproduction of any part may take place without the written
permission of Cambridge University Press.

First published 1993

A catalogue record for this publication is available from the British Library

National Library of Congress Cataloguing in Publication data
Summons, John, 1952—
Massacre at Myall Creek
Bibliography
ISBN 0 521 44763 1
1. College and school drama. 2. Aborigines, Australian — New South Wales—
Myall Creek — Treatment — Drama. 3. Massacres — New South Wales —
Myall Creek — Drama. I. Title
A822.3

Library of Congress Cataloguing in Publication data
Summons, John, 1952-
Massacre at Myall Creek / John Summons
p. cm.
Summary: A play about the massacre of Australian aborigines at Myall Creek in
New South Wales and the conviction of the whites charged with the killing.
ISBN 0-521-44763-1 Paperback
1. Australian aborigines—Australia—New South Wales—History—Juvenile
drama. 2. Massacres—Australia—New South Wales—History—Juvenile drama.
3. Young adult drama, Australian. [1. Australian aborigines—Drama. 2. Australia
—History—Drama. 3. Plays.]
I. Title
PR9619.3.S92M37   1993
822—dc20   93-21583
                                                                                                  CIP

ISBN 978-0-521-44763-8 paperback

Transferred to digital printing 2009

Cambridge University Press has no responsibility for the persistence or
accuracy of URLs for external or third-party Internet websites referred to in
this publication, and does not guarantee that any content on such websites is,
or will remain, accurate or appropriate. Information regarding prices, travel
timetables and other factual information given in this work are correct at
the time of first printing but Cambridge University Press does not guarantee
the accuracy of such information thereafter.

Contents

Introduction v

Massacre at Myall Creek 1
   Scene one 3
   Scene two 13
   Scene three 17
   Scene four 23
   Scene five 29
   Scene six 35
   Scene seven 43

Study units

English — Issues and themes 46
   Human violence 46
   Racism 46
   Displacement 47
   Authority and power 48
   Justice 48
   Capital punishment 49
   Courage and personal responsibility 50

English — Language workshop 51

English and Drama — Literary and performance considerations 55
   Characterisation 55
   Style and performance 57
   Improvisations 58

History and Aboriginal Studies 60

Suggested reading 66

Australian Aborigines slaughtered by Convicts. In Camden Pelham, *The Chronicles of Crime*, v.2, 1886 (Mitchell Library, State Library of New South Wales)

Introduction

In 1838 violence between Aboriginal peoples and white people in Australia culminated in a series of massacres of Aboriginal people, including one at Myall Creek in the north-west of New South Wales. That this massacre received so much attention at the time was not because it provoked great public outrage at the death of so many Aborigines at the hands of whites, but because it coincided with the climax of another struggle in the colony, the struggle for power and land. Following the massacre, and in response to it, seven men were hanged by a government determined to take a stand. Such was the heat of the reaction, however, that these seven became the last to hang for such crimes. In the end little changed for Aboriginal people as they continued to be massacred and their land taken by the white invaders.

This, then, is the background of *Massacre at Myall Creek*. It shows the worst aspects of the white society at the time — its greed, its selfishness, its wanton disregard for human life. The play, however, is not intended simply to be a litany of evil deeds, but attempts to explore in a dramatic way the social and political climate in which these and other massacres took place. In doing so, it seeks to examine the attitudes and policies that led to such inhumanity and to pose questions of ongoing and universal relevance.

The play, as presented here, is in the form in which it appears as a theatre-in-education piece touring schools in the Sydney metropolitan area. As such it is designed for two actors, each playing a number of roles. It can also be easily broken into parts for the purpose of a classroom reading or performance.

The study units that follow the play include work on themes and issues raised by the play, a language workshop based on the play, and literary and dramatic considerations, as well as activities dealing with historical matters. The units are aimed at those interested in English, drama, history, geography and Aboriginal studies. They are also suitable for those who prefer an across-curricula approach.

It should also be noted that the play essentially follows the events that occurred after the massacre and that these events are therefore viewed from the perspective of the white characters in the drama — convicts, landowners and government officials — and not that of the Aboriginal victims of the massacre. Because of this, I strongly recommend teachers acquaint their students with those parts of the study units (in English, history and drama) designed to help students gain an Aboriginal perspective of the events. I also suggest that teachers acquaint their students with those aspects of the study unit 'Language workshop', which provide an understanding of the language used in the play, especially language that may be considered derogatory towards Aboriginal people. It is important that students realise that such language is used in the drama to reflect accurately the white colonial attitudes of the time and that its usage is in no way acceptable today.

John Summons

Characters

NARRATOR 1:

   George ANDERSON, convict, aged 24.

   William HOBBS, overseer, aged 26.

   Sir George GIPPS, Governor of the colony, aged 47.

NARRATOR 2:

   Charles KILMEISTER, convict, aged 23.

   John PLUNKETT, Attorney-General, aged 36.

   Henry DANGAR, landowner, aged 42.

   Robert SCOTT, landowner, aged 39.

Production note

The play is performed by two actors playing a number of roles each. The play is intended to be done with a minimum of costumes. The two actors wear black jeans and shirts throughout the play to which they add one or two pieces of costume to suggest the essentials of each character. There is a costume rack on stage which is visible to the audience. The audience watches the actors change into their costumes. The actors also set up the stage furniture for the various scenes during the narration passages.

   Stage furniture necessary to the play is simple: a small camp stool to represent the convicts' hut; a desk and two chairs to represent the Governor's office. Other scenes in the play take place on a bare stage.

NARRATION ONE

NARRATOR 1: When Britain took possession of the continent of Australia, it was declared 'terra nullius' — belonging to no-one. That large numbers of Aboriginal people occupied the land went unheeded, despite the fact they sometimes fought and in other ways resisted the white invaders. The Aboriginal people of Australia were to become invisible to their white colonisers, no-account people who had had their day and whom time, disease and murder would now finally eradicate. The massacre at Myall Creek was one such eradication. It was not the biggest massacre, but it was perhaps one of the most significant, something of a watershed in what passed for black and white relations.

But let us begin. The time is Saturday, June the 10th, 1838. The place, Henry Dangar's Myall Creek property in the north-west of New South Wales. It is sunset, and two convict stockmen, Charles Kilmeister and George Anderson, rest in their hut. Outside, around a camp-fire, some Aboriginal people from the Weraerai clan — mostly women, children and old men — cook their meal and make ready for the night.

Scene one

[*Convicts' hut, Mr Dangar's Myall Creek property.* ANDERSON *sits on a small wooden stool, wrapped in a blanket.* KILMEISTER *stands at an imaginary door looking at the Aboriginal camp in the distance.*]

KILMEISTER: [*looking out*] Cunning devil.

ANDERSON: [*trying to get warm by wrapping himself in a blanket*] What?

KILMEISTER: I said, he's a cunning devil.

ANDERSON: Who?

KILMEISTER: Who do you think? Old Daddy.

ANDERSON: He's the biggest black I've ever seen.

KILMEISTER: Cured a woman just by singing to her.

ANDERSON: What are you doing?

KILMEISTER: Just watching the sun go down.

ANDERSON: Well, close the door, Kilmeister. It's cold in here.

KILMEISTER: Ah, you're always complaining, Anderson.

ANDERSON: This hut's draughty enough without the door open.

MASSACRE AT MYALL CREEK

KILMEISTER: If you'd cut some wood today we'd have had a fire.

ANDERSON: Yeah, well I didn't get around to it.

KILMEISTER: What did you do all day? Wear a hole in the bed?

ANDERSON: A man's entitled to a rest.

KILMEISTER: You're cocky now, but if Hobbs was here you'd soon change your ways. If Hobbs heard you spent the day on your back —

ANDERSON: What Hobbs doesn't know won't hurt him. Will it, Charlie?

KILMEISTER: Were you alone?

ANDERSON: Might have been. What's it to you?

KILMEISTER: Nothing. Except I've been out there all day riding my rump raw while you've been back here having fun.

ANDERSON: You didn't have to go. Nothing would've happened.

KILMEISTER: But if it had, Hobbs would've had my neck. The blacks could've driven off the cattle.

ANDERSON: These blacks wouldn't do anything. Anyway, most of the menfolk have gone. Mr Foster from Newton's station took a mob of them to cut bark.

KILMEISTER: Yeah, but you can't be too careful. If anything did happen we'd be the ones who'd get punished for letting it happen.

SCENE ONE

ANDERSON: I don't know, Charlie. What's the use of Hobbs going away if you're not going to enjoy yourself? Why are you afraid of him?

KILMEISTER: I'm not afraid of him.

ANDERSON: Even when he's not here you act like he is.

KILMEISTER: Ah! [*pause*] I wonder what they're cooking. Smells good. [*pause*] The camp will be quieter tonight with their men gone. Just the women, the children and the old men left.

ANDERSON: And you and me.

KILMEISTER: There are some good-looking gins in this mob.

ANDERSON: Fancy one yourself, do you?

KILMEISTER: Me? Wouldn't touch one. Hey, there's young Charlie. [*shouting*] Come here, Charlie!

ANDERSON: What are you doing now?

KILMEISTER: It's Charlie. [*loudly*] Charlie, come here! [*to* ANDERSON] He likes being called after me. You've seen the way he follows me about — like a dog.

ANDERSON: He follows anyone around. Even follows Hobbs. Hobbs doesn't seem to mind. In fact, I think he likes it. Funny, I didn't think Hobbs would like blacks, but he likes Charlie.

KILMEISTER: Young Charlie might follow him about, but he likes me best. I teach him things. I'm teaching him to talk. Catches on fast. Says everything I say — just like a parrot. Real smart — for a black.

[*Anderson gets off the bed and goes over to the doorway and looks out.*]

ANDERSON: Doesn't take much notice of you.

KILMEISTER: Ah, he can't hear me, that's all. [*roaring*] Charlie!

ANDERSON: Come on now, close the door.

KILMEISTER: Wait. [*pause*] Do you hear that?

ANDERSON: What?

KILMEISTER: Listen.

[ANDERSON *listens.*]

ANDERSON: I can't hear anything. [*indicating the camp*] Except them.

KILMEISTER: No, in the distance. Horses.

ANDERSON: [*listening again*] Nothing. I don't hear anything.

KILMEISTER: Someone's riding this way. No. Not just one. There's a lot of them.

ANDERSON: How can you tell?

KILMEISTER: Listen!

ANDERSON: You're imagining things, Kilmeister. Come on, let's close the door.

SCENE ONE

[ANDERSON *closes the door.*]

KILMEISTER: I swear I heard horses.

ANDERSON: Look, my hearing's as good as yours and I heard nothing. [*pacing to keep warm*] You're going mad, Charlie.

KILMEISTER: I'm not going mad! I heard something. [*uncertain*] I'm sure I did.

ANDERSON: Hey, I was only joking, Charlie. Out here you imagine things all the time. It's because we're away from white folk with all these blacks. Your mind plays tricks on you. You think you see things, you think you hear things, but it's not real. Don't take any notice of it, Charlie, or you will go mad. [*pause*] I wish I was out of here.

KILMEISTER: Where? In government service? No. At least out here we're free.

ANDERSON: Yeah, we're free. There's nowhere to escape, even if we wanted to. There's nothing but bush and blacks.

KILMEISTER: No, Anderson, here we're as free as a convict can be. There's Hobbs, I know, but he's not bad. I've known worse overseers.

ANDERSON: Yeah, Hobbs is all right. But it's not that. It's the loneliness, Charlie. Sometimes I get so lonely I think I'd rather be dead.

KILMEISTER: Well, I'm happy, even if you're not. We're here for the rest of our lives, we've got to make the best of it. You can't fight it. As

	long as you do what you're told and stay out of trouble, you'll have no worries.
ANDERSON:	You mean spend the rest of our lives cringing, tails between our legs, like whipped curs?
KILMEISTER:	Well, making trouble won't get you anything. Except a flogging. That's what's wrong with you, Anderson, you're not content. You just have to make trouble.
ANDERSON:	Ah! What are you talking about? What trouble have I caused?
KILMEISTER:	You and that gin.
ANDERSON:	What about me and Ipeta?
KILMEISTER:	It'll cause trouble. That kind of thing always causes trouble.
ANDERSON:	I like her and she likes me. What's wrong with that? Anyway, what business is it of yours?
KILMEISTER:	Damn you, Anderson, you'll cause trouble not only for yourself, but me! Don't forget it was me who talked Hobbs into letting the blacks camp here.
ANDERSON:	Nothing's going to happen.
KILMEISTER:	Those blackfellas won't let you play around with their women for nothing. They'll expect you to pay. And you better give them what they want.
ANDERSON:	Nothing will happen, I tell you.

SCENE ONE

KILMEISTER: Yeah, they're friendly enough now, but you wait. I don't trust them.

ANDERSON: If you don't trust them, why did you talk Hobbs into letting them stay?

KILMEISTER: They're all right as long as you leave their women alone.

ANDERSON: That still doesn't explain why you wanted them to stay.

KILMEISTER: For a bit of fun. A bit of noise. Sometimes it gets a bit quiet around here. And, I guess, like you, I get a bit lonely at times. [*suddenly becoming alert*] Listen!

ANDERSON: What now?

KILMEISTER: Horses. I hear horses again.

ANDERSON: Ah, Charlie.

KILMEISTER: Someone's coming.

ANDERSON: Who? Look, I told you—

KILMEISTER: Listen! [*pause*] It's real, I'm not just imagining.

[*They both listen intently.*]

ANDERSON: I can hear something.

KILMEISTER: See!

ANDERSON: All right, all right. But who do you think it is?

KILMEISTER: I don't know.

ANDERSON: Hobbs and the men?

KILMEISTER: They won't be back for a couple of days. Anyway, there's too many of them.

ANDERSON: How do you know that?

KILMEISTER: [*shrugging*] I just know.

ANDERSON: Well, who are they then? Charlie? Who are they?

[KILMEISTER *doesn't answer, he merely shrugs his shoulders.*]

[*urgently*] Charlie?

KILMEISTER: I don't know, I tell you! But something's wrong. I can feel it. I always know when there's going to be trouble.

ANDERSON: I don't like it, Charlie. What's going on?

[KILMEISTER *doesn't answer, but sits down slowly on his stool. He stares at the floor solemnly.*]

I'm going out to take a look.

[ANDERSON *goes to the door, but stops to regard* KILMEISTER, *who now gazes at the palm of his hand.*]

What's wrong with you?

KILMEISTER: I see blood.

[KILMEISTER *and* ANDERSON *look at one another, their faces frozen in bewilderment and fear.*]

NARRATION TWO

NARRATOR 2: Several days later, William Hobbs, station overseer at Myall Creek, made his way back from Dangar's lower station on the Gwydir River, sixty miles to the west. On his journey home to Myall Creek he learnt that a brutal massacre of twenty-eight Aborigines had taken place at the Myall Creek property. He decided to investigate the report, searching the property on his return. Guided to the spot of the massacre he found the butchered and burnt remains of the twenty-eight Aboriginal people. He then began questioning his men, Anderson and Kilmeister. They, however, proved tight-lipped and evasive, a strange mood having overcome them. They now seemed extremely tense with a stronger than usual antagonism existing between them.

Scene two

[ANDERSON *and* KILMEISTER *outside the hut.*]

ANDERSON: Hobbs wants to see you, Kilmeister.

KILMEISTER: I know. I heard him calling. What does he want now?

ANDERSON: You better go, Charlie.

KILMEISTER: Hasn't he asked enough questions? What did he ask you?

ANDERSON: Nothing.

KILMEISTER: He must've asked you something, you were with him long enough. Did he ask you about me?

ANDERSON: Yeah.

KILMEISTER: And what did you say?

ANDERSON: Nothing, I told you. I said I didn't know anything.

KILMEISTER: Are you sure that's all you said? You know what'll happen to you if you've opened your mouth?

ANDERSON: I'm not frightened of you.

KILMEISTER: But it's not just me you've got to be frightened of, is it?

ANDERSON: Why did you do it, Charlie? Why did you join them?

KILMEISTER: I was afraid. I didn't know what they were going to do. I thought they were only going to scare the blacks.

ANDERSON: Scare them? Is that what you call it? [*grabbing* KILMEISTER *around the throat*] I ought to kill you, Charlie! I ought to squeeze the miserable life out of you! Ah, what's the use?

[*He pushes* KILMEISTER *away.*]

KILMEISTER: [*gasping*] God, you near strangled me.

ANDERSON: I hope they get you, Charlie. I hope they get the lot of you.

KILMEISTER: No-one's going to get us. No-one's going to do anything over a few blacks.

ANDERSON: Then why are you worried?

KILMEISTER: I'm not worried. It's just that Hobbs won't let it be. Why won't he let it rest? I don't understand him. Anyway, even Hobbs can't do anything if no-one will talk.
[*pause*] You won't speak against us, Anderson? [*pause*]
Well?

ANDERSON: I don't know.

KILMEISTER: You can't speak against us, Anderson. You're a convict, you're one of us. If you speak against us it'll only be helping them punish your own kind. Why help them?

SCENE TWO

	You don't owe them anything. What do you owe them? Nothing!
ANDERSON:	Shut up, Charlie.
KILMEISTER:	You won't speak against us, will you? Not against your own kind.
ANDERSON:	I said, I don't know. You better go now, Hobbs will be getting angry.
KILMEISTER:	Don't speak against us. Please, don't speak against us.
ANDERSON:	And why not? What do I owe you? You killed Ipeta.
KILMEISTER:	I had nothing to do with that. It wasn't my fault. It was the others, the others. Blame them.
ANDERSON:	Go! Get away from me!

[*He pushes* KILMEISTER *away, then marches off.*]

15

NARRATION THREE

NARRATOR 1: Hobbs had become angry and impatient at his men's reluctance to reveal what they knew. Both men, he was sure, knew far more than they were telling. Now it was Kilmeister's turn to be interrogated again. Hobbs was determined this time to get at the truth.

Scene three

[*Inside the hut.* HOBBS *sits on the stool, smoking a pipe.*]

HOBBS: You took your time. You come when I call you.

KILMEISTER: Sorry, Mr Hobbs.

HOBBS: What took you so long?

KILMEISTER: Oh. I was telling Anderson what needed to be done. That Anderson's so lazy, Mr Hobbs, if you don't tell him exactly what's to be done, he won't do it. He'll be off asleep somewhere. He needs watching, that one. If I were you, Mr Hobbs, I'd —

HOBBS: All right. Enough. Do you know why you're here?

KILMEISTER: No, sir.

HOBBS: Come now, Kilmeister, you know very well why you're here.

KILMEISTER: Would it be about the blacks, sir?

HOBBS: Of course it's about the blacks! Now I want to know precisely what happened. Everything.

KILMEISTER: But I've told you everything, Mr Hobbs.

HOBBS: Then I am dissatisfied with your explanation. How could you have allowed this to happen? These blacks were your friends, yet you did nothing to save them. Furthermore, and this I simply cannot understand, I have reason to believe that you took part in the atrocities.

KILMEISTER: No, sir! That's a lie! Did Anderson say that? Anderson's a liar! You don't believe Anderson?

HOBBS: What's wrong?

KILMEISTER: You don't want to believe anything that Anderson says. He's a lazy, lying —

HOBBS: I never mentioned Anderson.

KILMEISTER: No, sir.

HOBBS: Well, did you?

KILMEISTER: No, sir! I told you —

HOBBS: Come on, Kilmeister, you were seen later with these murderers at Newton's Station, looking for blacks there.

KILMEISTER: I was there looking for stray cattle. The blacks rushed the cattle and scared them off.

HOBBS: When I rode in the cattle were all right. You're not telling the truth.

KILMEISTER: I am, sir!

HOBBS: You're not! You also claim that you did not recognise any of these men.

SCENE THREE

KILMEISTER: Yes, sir.

HOBBS: But you rode in their company.

KILMEISTER: Yes, sir.

HOBBS: How can that be?

KILMEISTER: It's true, Mr Hobbs, I swear.

HOBBS: Look, it might go easier for you if you tell the truth. This is serious business.

KILMEISTER: I am telling the truth.

HOBBS: Of course you realise Mr Dangar will have to be informed of what's happened?

KILMEISTER: Mr Dangar?

HOBBS: As owner of this property he must be informed, and as his overseer it is my duty to do so.

KILMEISTER: Don't tell Mr Dangar. You don't need to tell Mr Dangar.

HOBBS: If you are telling the truth, you'll have nothing to fear.

KILMEISTER: He'll blame me for the cattle.

HOBBS: [*exasperated*] The cattle again.

KILMEISTER: He'll say I wasn't doing my job. That I let the blacks spear some cattle. He'll blame me for that.

HOBBS: The blacks speared some cattle? You said they rushed the cattle and scared them off, you've said nothing about them spearing cattle.

KILMEISTER: I —

HOBBS: All right, Kilmeister, if the blacks speared some cattle, there should be carcasses. You and I are going to ride this property until we find them. We'll soon learn if you're telling the truth.

KILMEISTER: Yes, sir. [*pause*] Do you really need to tell Mr Dangar?

HOBBS: I have no choice.

KILMEISTER: Don't tell him.

HOBBS: I must.

KILMEISTER: He'll put me into government service.

HOBBS: Not if you're innocent. [*pause*] Look, Kilmeister, we are not just talking of the possible killing of cattle, we are talking of the actual slaughter of helpless women, children and old men — twenty-eight innocent human beings! And let me warn you, if you're found party to that crime, you'll have more to fear than government service. You'll hang!

KILMEISTER: Please, Mr Hobbs, for Lord Jesus Christ sake, don't report it!

[*He goes down on his knees.*]

HOBBS: What are you doing?

KILMEISTER: I beg you, Mr Hobbs. Please.

HOBBS: Off your knees, man.

SCENE THREE

KILMEISTER: I'm innocent! I'm innocent! Have mercy on me. Please.

HOBBS: Like you had mercy on the blacks?

KILMEISTER: I had nothing to do with that, I swear to God.

HOBBS: You didn't even have the decency to bury their remains.

KILMEISTER: I'll bury their bodies if you like.

HOBBS: If you are innocent as you claim that would only do you harm. You're not to go near those bodies, you hear. I want them left exactly as they are.

KILMEISTER: Yes, sir.

HOBBS: Now get up off your knees. An innocent man, Kilmeister, has no need to beg.

KILMEISTER: Sir.

[*Kilmeister stands slowly.*]

HOBBS: You are beginning to show the signs of a man with an over-burdened conscience.

KILMEISTER: Will there be anything else?

HOBBS: What?

KILMEISTER: Can I go now, Mr Hobbs?

HOBBS: [*sighing*] Yes — go. [*pause*] You know, Kilmeister, I'm sorry I ever let you talk me into allowing those blacks to stay.

KILMEISTER: I'm sorry, too. I knew those blacks would cause trouble. I knew it.

NARRATION FOUR

NARRATOR 2: News of the massacre reached Sydney, causing a dilemma for the recently appointed Governor Gipps, who, like the governors before him, was faced with many problems in the young colony, torn as it was with divisions of class, race and religion: free settler versus ex-convict, Irish versus English, Catholic versus Protestant. Life for the Governor was a constant balancing act between these conflicting forces, each demanding attention to their grievances, each trying to win him to their cause, each trying to challenge his authority. Now to add to the Governor's problems was the issue of black versus white, brought to a head by a number of serious conflicts in which large numbers of Aboriginal people and small numbers of squatters had been killed.

To further complicate the Governor's position he had recently been ordered by London to give equal protection to both Aboriginal people and colonists. This meant that no longer could whites and blacks kill each other freely. The law demanded that any transgressor be tried and punished. Now, with this latest massacre at Myall Creek, the Governor had to decide if those responsible should be arrested and prosecuted. If found guilty, white men would hang for killing Aboriginal people — an almost unprecedented event, and one which Governor Gipps feared might provoke an unpredictable, perhaps dangerous, reaction. Keen to act on the issue, but careful to make the right decision, he turned to his Attorney-General, an Irishman, John Herbert Plunkett, for his advice.

Scene four

[GOVERNOR GIPPS' *office. It consists essentially of a desk and two chairs.* GIPPS *sits behind the desk and* PLUNKETT *opposite him.*]

GIPPS: I am but new to the colony. You know these matters better than I. As Attorney-General, Mr Plunkett, what is your advice?

PLUNKETT: I can only advise Your Excellency that you do your duty. The orders from London are most clear on this point — the Aborigine must be given the same protection as the white. If such a crime has been committed, it must be investigated and those guilty brought to trial.

GIPPS: I agree with you, Mr Plunkett, but would it not be wiser to wait? Feeling against the blacks is strong at present. And I'm afraid that while Aborigines continue to murder whites, the public will not punish white men for doing the same.

PLUNKETT: The law is the law, it must be applied equally to all.

GIPPS: Yes, the law is the law, but its application is a matter for the most prudent judgement. To take such action now may only increase hostility between the races.

PLUNKETT:	[*standing*] You must take action!
GIPPS:	I must, Mr Plunkett? Must I remind you that I am Governor? I asked for your advice, not your command.
PLUNKETT:	I intended no disrespect, sir. I merely wished to impress upon Your Excellency the urgency of the matter. These outrages by both black and white must come to an end. And only firm action by Your Excellency can achieve that.
GIPPS:	I know my duty and I will act as I see fit.
PLUNKETT:	But sir, if we delay any longer the situation can only get worse. The colony is growing at a rate the Government cannot control. With every new expansion the Aborigine is further displaced and conflict increased. How can law and order be maintained when the Government lacks effective control? We can only rely on the good will of unscrupulous men whose sole motivation is the greed for more land. For too long this colony has been ruled by such men, wealthy men, who have no regard for the rights of others and who have become a law unto themselves. No, sir, it is not good enough! The Government must assert its authority, the law must be upheld! Otherwise, there will be anarchy.
GIPPS:	You speak with passion.

SCENE FOUR

PLUNKETT: Only because I believe that if we are ever to have a free society, there must be equality for all, regardless of race, creed or colour. We are all God's children and equal in His sight.

GIPPS: These are noble sentiments. You are a religious man?

PLUNKETT: I am a Christian. As is Your Excellency.

GIPPS: A Catholic?

PLUNKETT: Yes, sir. A Catholic is a Christian.

GIPPS: I was not suggesting anything to the contrary. You are very sensitive to the subject, Mr Plunkett.

PLUNKETT: I know that many resent having a Catholic as Attorney-General.

GIPPS: I believe you are the first Catholic in the colony to have achieved such a high office.

PLUNKETT: Yes, sir. And I am sure in the years to come there will be many others who will achieve the same.

GIPPS: No doubt.

PLUNKETT: I am determined that there will. But why do you ask these questions, Your Excellency?

GIPPS: I am not a man of passion, Mr Plunkett, I am a man of reason. When I sought your advice it was to find practical solutions to practical problems. And while I admire your convictions I must know that your advice is based on sound reasoning and not influenced by some sense of injured pride over personal attacks on your character and religion.

PLUNKETT: Sir, I can assure you, I care only for the welfare of the colony. I want what all true Christians want, a society that will not tolerate evil, but pluck it from men's hearts wherever it exists. And that is why I say we must act now. The squatters and landowners must not be allowed to further their corruption. They and their men must be taught that a black's life is as worthwhile as a white's and that they cannot murder with impunity.

GIPPS: Yes — I agree, but as I have said, there are practical considerations. We must find the best strategy to meet our objectives.

PLUNKETT: You must do something!

GIPPS: It seems you are going to make a habit of giving me orders!

PLUNKETT: They will have you under their thumb! I'm sorry, Your Excellency, but I must speak out.

GIPPS: You are making me angry, Mr Plunkett. I am not a man to be intimidated.

PLUNKETT: Then you must show them, or you will lose all authority.

SCENE FOUR

GIPPS: That's enough, Mr Plunkett! [*cooling down*] Let us return to the business at hand. And I hope you will conduct yourself in a more reasonable manner. Sit down.

[PLUNKETT *sits down. He looks a little indignant.*]

Now, Mr Plunkett, this report from the Police Magistrate at Muswellbrook, concerning an alleged atrocity at Mr Dangar's Myall Creek property — you would advise me to have the Magistrate investigate it?

PLUNKETT: Yes, sir, I do. Without delay.

GIPPS: Good. So be it. But let me warn you — I do this not to please you. I will be under no-one's thumb — including yours. You will see, Mr Plunkett, that in this colony I am the authority.

NARRATION FIVE

NARRATOR 1: In late July 1838 the Police Magistrate, Edward Day, arrived at Myall Creek to investigate the massacre. By the time he left the district he had arrested eleven men for the crime. Of these, six were convicts: Charles Kilmeister, Charles Toulouse, Edward Foley, John Blake, James Parry and James Oates. Two were ticket-of-leave men: William Hawkins and Charles Lamb. Three were ex-convicts: George Palliser, John Russell and John Johnston, the latter a Negro. A twelfth man, John Fleming, a ringleader and the son of a local landowner, managed to escape.

NARRATOR 2: Henry Dangar, controversial owner of Myall Creek Station, having heard reports of the massacre, made his way to Muswelbrook to speak with the Police Magistrate about the incident.

Henry Dangar was well known in the colony. In 1827 he had been dismissed from his position as assistant Surveyor of Lands for wrongfully acquiring large tracts of prime land for himself and his brother. Despite this setback, however, he eventually became a wealthy landowner and a man of influence.

When Dangar talked to the Police Magistrate about the massacre he learnt much that did not please him, although he did his best to hide his displeasure. How absurd, he thought, to make such a fuss over the massacre of a few blacks! Why, these men had simply done their duty — ridding the countryside of a troublesome pest. No, he would stand by Kilmeister — a loyal servant deserved a loyal master. There was one problem, however — Hobbs. Dangar was particularly annoyed that his overseer had brought the massacre to light and had now become a principal witness for the prosecution.

In early October, with the trial of the eleven men pending, Dangar decided to ride to his Myall Creek property to confront Hobbs and to make his feelings known to his overseer about the matter.

Scene five

[*Outside the hut.* DANGAR *and* HOBBS *stand.* DANGAR *has a somewhat forced smile upon his face.*]

DANGAR: Well, well, Hobbs. It seems congratulations are in order. When I spoke to the Police Magistrate in Muswelbrook, he informed me that his visit here had been most productive. Yes, he appeared most pleased with his catch.

HOBBS: Yes, but it was not easy. Many were against him.

DANGAR: And he was wise taking Anderson into protective custody. Anderson will need protection now.

HOBBS: Anderson's coming forward made it easier. Surprised me, though. I didn't think the lad had it in him.

DANGAR: Yes, but much of the credit must go to you, Hobbs. It was mainly through your efforts that they were caught. You should be pleased with yourself, too.

HOBBS: I take no pleasure in it, Mr Dangar. I was only doing my duty.

DANGAR:	[*dropping his smile and suddenly turning on* HOBBS] If only you had taken more care in your duties as my overseer.
HOBBS:	Sir?
DANGAR:	If you had not allowed the blacks to camp on the property this whole situation could have been avoided.
HOBBS:	Yes, sir. But these blacks had caused no trouble, not here, or at the other stations they'd camped at. They were known in the district for being peaceable and well behaved. I would not have allowed them to stay otherwise.
DANGAR:	Is there such a thing as a peaceable, well-behaved black? There are to be no blacks on the property, and if there are, action is to be taken. You know as well as I do the trouble the blacks have caused.
HOBBS:	Not these blacks, Mr Dangar. They were perfectly tame. They even did work for us.
DANGAR:	Perfectly tame? Are you sure you were not fooled? The native has the cunning of an animal. He is by his nature deceptive and treacherous. Given time, I'm sure the true nature of these blacks would have revealed itself. You disappoint me, Hobbs, I thought you were a reliable man.
HOBBS:	[*meekly*] Sir.
DANGAR:	And why was I not notified of this incident before the Police Magistrate?

SCENE FIVE

HOBBS: I was unable to reach you, Mr Dangar. I thought someone in authority should know.

DANGAR: I am your authority, Hobbs. I am owner of this property and your first duty is to me. We don't want the law poking around in our affairs.

HOBBS: But we have nothing to hide. And if our men have committed these crimes they should be punished.

DANGAR: There are ways of handling such things without involving the law.

HOBBS: I did what I thought was best, sir.

[DANGAR *looks a*t HOBBS *a moment, studies him, then sighs.*]

DANGAR: Oh well, what's done is done. Perhaps I am being too hard on you. After all, I've never had reason to complain of your conduct before. Up until now you have been a most satisfactory overseer.

HOBBS: [*appreciatively*] Sir.

DANGAR: Yes, you're a good man, Hobbs. When the Police Magistrate inquired, I assured him you were of excellent character.

HOBBS: Thank you, sir.

DANGAR: And fortunately, even now, all is not lost. You may still have the opportunity to make amends.

HOBBS: I don't understand, Mr Dangar.

DANGAR: The trial. There is still the trial, don't forget.

HOBBS: Yes. But I don't see —

DANGAR: Your evidence will no doubt be of great importance to the case.

HOBBS: It's not just my evidence, Mr Dangar, there are others.

DANGAR: But not so important as you.

HOBBS: There's Anderson.

DANGAR: Anderson? A convict? Who will believe the word of a convict against a man of such excellent character?

HOBBS: Sir? Do you mean I should perjure myself? I cannot perjure myself, Mr Dangar.

DANGAR: I'm not suggesting that you perjure yourself. I was merely going to suggest that you be certain of your evidence. You are human, you can make mistakes. Perhaps there is something you've overlooked. Something that may cause you to change your mind. Now, our man Kilmeister, for instance, perhaps —

HOBBS: Sir, I carefully examined Kilmeister's claims and found them without substance. Kilmeister is a liar, sir.

DANGAR: But the overall evidence against these men is slim indeed, Hobbs. Why, there aren't even any bodies.

SCENE FIVE

HOBBS: No, sir. They managed to remove the bodies before the Police Magistrate could examine them.

DANGAR: There then, you see? What real evidence is there?

HOBBS: But surely the fact that the bodies were removed only confirms their guilt?

DANGAR: The act of desperate men wrongly accused of a crime. How can you be so certain they are guilty, Hobbs? You don't want to cause innocent men to be punished. Think carefully. If there is even the remotest possibility of doubt in your mind, it is your duty, as a conscientious man, to give them the benefit of the doubt.

HOBBS: Sir, I must tell the truth.

DANGAR: Yes, of course you must. Only think over what I have said. It may be in your interest to give deeper thought to the matter.

HOBBS: Sir?

DANGAR: Your term of employment — it expires soon?

HOBBS: Yes, sir.

DANGAR: Then soon I may no longer require your services. And I would regard it a great pity to lose such a good man.

NARRATION SIX

NARRATOR 1: Concern for the fate of the eleven arrested men grew among many landowners and other sections in the colony as it became evident that these men not only faced a trial, but also the prospect of hanging. In response, the squatters of the Hunter River Valley and Liverpool Plains, including Henry Dangar, formed a semi-secret organisation called the Hunter River Black Association to give support to the prisoners and contribute money for their defence, hiring the three best lawyers in Sydney.

NARRATOR 2: The chairman of the Hunter River Black Association was Robert Scott, a wealthy landowner and magistrate. Scott visited the eleven men in gaol and advised them to stick together, to say nothing and admit nothing as there was no direct evidence against them. This was a very unusual action for a man in the position of a magistrate to take. Governor Gipps, who was now determined to take action over the Myall Creek incident, received a report on Scott's visit to the gaol and the advice Scott had given. Later, Scott called on the Governor to explain his actions and state his case.

Scene six

[GIPPS' *office.* GIPPS *stands behind his desk, pacing a little.* SCOTT *sits opposite him.*]

GIPPS: This is astounding, Mr Scott, that you, a magistrate, should have taken such action. Do you deny speaking with these men in prison?

SCOTT: I do not deny speaking with these men, Your Excellency, nor giving them advice.

GIPPS: But surely you realise the seriousness of the matter?

SCOTT: That is why I am here, Your Excellency. To apologise.

GIPPS: Apologise?

SCOTT: Yes, Your Excellency. I would not have spoken as I did if I had realised at the time that there was evidence of any substance against these men. Since then, however, I have had the opportunity of reading the investigating Police Magistrate's report in which I see that some evidence does exist, although it is far from conclusive in my opinion.

GIPPS: I see. Nevertheless, Mr Scott, such action may have done irreparable harm to their case. Anyway, for the moment I'll speak no more on the matter. I hope, however, in the future you will refrain from taking such actions.

SCOTT: But I must do everything that I can to save these men, Your Excellency. I and many other landholders in the district feel —

GIPPS: [*sitting down*] Yes, I know how you all feel — I have read your petition.

SCOTT: Well, Your Excellency?

GIPPS: What, Mr Scott? What more is to be said? It is now for the court to decide. These men will receive a fair trial.

SCOTT: Ah, what's the point! It is useless to appeal to the Government in this or anything! The Government turns a deaf ear to the concerns of landowners.

GIPPS: Pray, Mr Scott, what have I said to so upset you?

SCOTT: The issue is of greater importance than just the fate of these eleven men. There is a matter of principle involved. The Government encourages settlement, yet does nothing to protect us. Incidents such as these could be avoided if the Government would assume its responsibility and act against marauding blacks.

SCENE SIX

GIPPS: I will, of course, do all I can, but surely you understand that in such matters my hands are tied. We are not at war with the Aborigine.

SCOTT: These savages slaughter our sheep and cattle, murder our men. Are not these provocations acts of war? If it continues we may be forced to desert our runs. Is that Your Excellency's wish?

GIPPS: No. But you must realise the situation is complicated. The Aborigine naturally resents being forced from his land.

SCOTT: His land? But it is not his land. The Government recognises no legal title of the native to the land. The land belongs to those who make best use of it. The native, through his laziness and unprofitable use of the land, has forfeited that right and deserves to be dispossessed.

GIPPS: But surely, Mr Scott, as the original inhabitant of the soil, some consideration must be given to the welfare of the Aborigine?

SCOTT: Your Excellency, the time has come for us to take a stand. The native must be taught that the land is ours, that we are here to stay and that resistance is useless. And the sooner that lesson is taught, the better — for all concerned.

GIPPS: But, Mr Scott —

SCOTT: Your Excellency, we can't afford to be soft with these savages! In the past, force has been the only effective way of stopping their aggressions.

GIPPS: Yes, with the result that for the handful of whites killed by blacks in your district, hundreds of Aborigines have been slaughtered.

SCOTT: Which simply proves my point — we are outnumbered.

GIPPS: You're not serious?

SCOTT: We are few, they are many. That is the simple fact of the matter.

GIPPS: The simple fact?

SCOTT: Yes, Your Excellency, and unless we show them that we are prepared to take drastic action they will not respect us, or the laws of a civilised nation.

GIPPS: But I have told you, I cannot do as you ask. These people are, after all, British subjects too.

SCOTT: British subjects! It's a black day indeed when the British Government grants membership to baboons!

GIPPS: I do not make the policies, Mr Scott, I merely enforce what my superiors in London decree. And they have seen fit to grant the Aborigine the same protection as the white. Indeed, they have charged me with the responsibility for that protection.

SCENE SIX

SCOTT: London! What does London know of the situation here? They will hold up the development of this colony with their mawkish sentimentality over these primitives.

GIPPS: That, sir, is something you must discuss with London. I have my orders — I cannot and will not disobey them.

SCOTT: What we need in this colony is leadership, true leadership! Someone with initiative and determination. Someone who is man enough to do what needs to be done, without wincing, and without all this womanly guff about the protection of murdering savages. I had hoped you would have been such a man. But I see I was wrong.

GIPPS: Is there no-one in this colony who will not tell me how to do my job?

SCOTT: If you would do your job properly there would be no complaint. All we ask is for a little protection.

GIPPS: Mr Scott, I cannot give you the protection you require. You have placed yourself outside my control. Even if I had ten times the soldiers I could still not guarantee your safety. It has been your greed for land that has led to this predicament.

SCOTT: Sir, I protest! The wealth of the colony depends on the securing of new grazing lands.

GIPPS:	The wealth of the colony, sir? The wealth of your own pockets.
SCOTT:	I did not come here to be insulted.
GIPPS:	You and a few others have tied up all the land in your district — and you want more.
SCOTT:	Men of enterprise must have incentive.
GIPPS:	Yes, but when will you be content?
SCOTT:	[standing] It is clear, Your Excellency, that I am only wasting my time. You refuse to take this matter seriously.
GIPPS:	You misjudge me, Mr Scott. I take this matter very seriously.
SCOTT:	You'll learn, like your predecessors, that we landowners are not to be played with. We are not without our influence.
GIPPS:	Is that a threat?
SCOTT:	It is a simple fact.
GIPPS:	Another simple fact. You seem very fond of simplicity, Mr Scott.
SCOTT:	On such occasions I believe in plain speaking.
GIPPS:	I have been very patient with you. I have heard your request, I have considered it carefully, and I have informed you of my decision.

SCENE SIX

SCOTT: I am not satisfied with your decision. I strongly urge you to reconsider If Your Excellency refuses to take action against black outrages in our district then we will be forced by circumstances to take the law into our own hands.

GIPPS: That, sir, would be a fatal error.

SCOTT: I speak, of course, not for myself or the other landowners. We are law-abiding citizens, but our servants, sir, they are mostly convicts and ex-convicts, undisciplined men, lacking the restraint of their masters.

GIPPS: If that is the case, then I advise you to warn your men that if they are convicted of murdering an Aborigine, they will hang. And if their masters should, through some lapse in their morality, encourage their men to commit such crimes, then they too shall share their fate.

SCOTT: Is that a threat, sir?

GIPPS: No, sir — a simple fact.

NARRATION SEVEN

NARRATOR 1: There were two trials dealing with the Myall Creek massacre. The first trial started on the 15th of November, 1838, and consisted mainly of eye-witness accounts of the aftermath of the massacre and the identification of those who took part.

NARRATOR 2: One difficulty faced by the Crown in prosecuting the eleven men was the fact that, despite the evidence of witnesses that twenty-eight Aborigines had been killed and their bodies burnt, little remained of those bodies that could be clearly identified. In the first trial, the eleven prisoners were charged only with murder of the large Aboriginal man known as Daddy, parts of whose body were reasonably recognisable.

Among those who gave evidence were Anderson and Hobbs, who spoke as witnesses for the Crown. Henry Dangar spoke on behalf of the defence.

Scene seven

[*Court.* ANDERSON, HOBBS *and* DANGAR *take turns to speak as if giving evidence.*]

ANDERSON: My name is George Anderson. I am an assigned servant. I have worked for Mr Dangar at his Myall Creek station for the last several months. Mr Hobbs is overseer there. In June, when Mr Hobbs was away, some men rode up to our hut on horseback. They were all armed with swords, muskets and pistols. I was with Kilmeister when they came. They were yelling and shouting and making the blacks afraid. Later they took the blacks and bound them with rope and led them some distance away. I did not see what happened to the blacks, although I heard some shots. Of those who rode to the hut that night were: Russell, Johnston, Oates, Foley,

[*His voice begins to fade as he changes costume to become* HOBBS]

Hawkins, Toulouse, Lamb, Parry.

HOBBS: I went to the place where the killings had taken place. There were dead bodies everywhere: the bodies of women, the bodies of children, many without their heads. Most had been in some way mutilated and burnt. The stench was overwhelming and made me sick. I tried to count the bodies, but it proved very difficult at first, owing to the dismemberment and the smell. The most I counted were twenty-eight, taking account of all the heads and all the parts. There was one body there I took to be Daddy's. It was very large, although again without a head. I am sure, though, it was Daddy's. Daddy was very big. In fact, he was the largest man I have ever met, black or white.

DANGAR: Kilmeister's character is exemplary — a most faithful, obedient and trustworthy servant. No master could ask for more. [*pause, then, as if answering a question*] I resent that! What is more natural than a master's concern for his servant? I and other masters must testify for our men. It is our duty. [*pause, then, as if answering a question*] Anderson and Hobbs? Yes, they are also my servants, but Anderson is of very poor character and forever telling lies. I would not believe a word he says, even under oath. As for Hobbs — well, I'll say nothing for him or against him. Hobbs is leaving my employ. His contract has expired.

NARRATION EIGHT

NARRATOR 1: After considering the evidence for fifteen minutes the jury returned their verdict — not guilty — much to the delight of many in the courtroom. One of the jury was later reported to have said: 'I would never consent to hang a white man for a black one. I knew well they were guilty of murder, but I, for one, would never see a white man suffer for shooting a black.'

The happy mood of the courtroom soon changed, however, when Attorney-General Plunkett announced that there would be a second trial. This time the men were charged with the murder of the Aboriginal child Charlie, or of an Aboriginal child unknown. This announcement of a second trial rocked the entire colony. Everyone had strong opinions on the matter.

NARRATOR 2: The second trial began on the 29th of November. Unlike the first, only seven of the eleven men stood trial, Attorney-General Plunkett giving the seven the opportunity to call the other four men as witnesses, since, as was custom at the time, those accused could not testify on their own behalf. Although the second trial presented similar evidence to the first, Plunkett pressed home an effective attack on the character of the defence witnesses, notably Henry Dangar, whose past dismissal from government office was used to undermine his credibility before the court. Finally the jury retired to consider its decision and returned with a verdict of guilty. The prisoners were later sentenced to death.

NARRATOR 1: Despite petitions for mercy the seven men were executed on the 18th of December. It was widely believed at the time that the Goverment was determined to make an example of these men.The remaining four never faced trial. As Governor Gipps was later to reveal in a report — the law had made its point.

NARRATOR 2: The Myall Creek massacre was but one of many massacres to have occurred since the coming of Europeans to Australia. Massacres, bigger and smaller, happened in many different parts of the land, in this century as well as last. Thus, in this and in other ways, have Aboriginal people lost both their lives and their land.

Study units

English — Issues and themes

The following are questions related to some of the important issues and themes raised by the play. The questions can be used in a number of ways, as topics for discussion or debate, or for essays. Not all questions need to be attempted by all students. Various aspects of each issue or theme can be handled by groups within the class and general conclusions reported back to the whole class. Reports may be of a factual kind or take the form of more imaginative responses by way of poems, short plays or short stories.

Human violence

1 Massacres usually occur when there is an atmosphere conducive to them. In times of war and civil unrest there are often massacres. What was it about the nature of the New South Wales colony in 1838 that was conducive to the Myall Creek massacre?

2 Sometimes massacres take place in 'the heat of the moment', as in the midst of a battle. Was the massacre at Myall Creek like this? How did it differ? How was the massacre at Myall Creek indicative of the larger campaign against Aboriginal people occurring at the time?

3 Can you think of other examples from history or today where massacres have been used systematically to achieve political ends?

4 The convict era in Australian history has often been described as being very brutal. How was the brutality of the times a contributing factor in the massacres that happened?

Racism

1 What is racism? Which characters in the play do you regard as having racist attitudes? Explain how these characters are racist in their attitudes.

2 How did racism contribute to the many massacres that occurred around the time of the Myall Creek massacre?

3 Do some white people regard themselves as superior to black people today? In what ways? What are your feelings about this?

4 Have you or someone you know ever experienced racism? Write your story.

5 Massacres still occur in many parts of the world. Some of these massacres are fuelled by racial tensions. Can such massacres be prevented? In our own society, how can such incidents be prevented? What is your role as an individual in this process?

Displacement

1 The process of displacement of the Aboriginal people in Australia began with the arrival of the Europeans. How in the play is this process demonstrated? Central to Aboriginal displacement and dispossession was the disregard by Europeans for Aboriginal rights to their land. In scene six the landowner Robert Scott states the Europeans' justification for this. What is his argument? What do you think of his reasons? What was the Government's position regarding Aboriginal land rights?

2 For a long time in Australian history European occupation of Australia has been referred to as European settlement. Today, however, many people say it should be called European invasion. Consider the words 'settlement' and 'invasion'. What ideas do we associate with each of these words? How have these two words been used historically and politically?

3 An invasion suggests warfare. Was there an official war between Aboriginal people and Europeans? Was there an unofficial war? What was Governor Gipps' view of the situation (see scene six)? Was Gipps' view realistic, given the many conflicts and massacres that took place at the time? (For an example of government involvement in atrocities against Aborigines find out what you can about 'Major Nunn's Campaign' of 1838.)

MASSACRE AT MYALL CREEK

4 For a long time the massacres and abuses of Aboriginal people by non-Aboriginal people have been omitted or downplayed in Australian history. What do you think have been the reasons for this?

5 What effects has this violent history had on the relationship between Aboriginal and non-Aboriginal people in contemporary Australian society?

6 Today, many Aboriginal people and fellow Australians are requesting that a treaty should be signed by the Government and the Aboriginal peoples, recognising the violent take-over of the country and the prior ownership of the land by Aboriginal people. What are your views on this?

Authority and power

1 An important theme in the play is the issue of authority and power. How is this theme brought out in the play? What is a 'power struggle'? Which characters in the play are interested in power struggles and questions of authority? (Refer to scenes four and six.)

2 In scene five, Hobbs told Dangar that he notified the authorities about the massacre because someone in authority should know. Dangar responded by telling Hobbs that he was Hobbs' authority. Both men used the word 'authority', but with different meanings. What did each man mean by this word?

Justice

1 How is the issue of justice brought out in the play? Which characters are interested in justice? Compare Plunkett's view of justice with Scott's. Are their views the same? What is Gipps' attitude to justice? (See scenes four and six.) In the play, how do political issues impinge on issues of justice?

2 It was reported in *The Australian,* 8 December 1838, that one juror said, after the first Myall Creek trial in which the men were acquitted, that he knew the men were guilty of murder, but that he

would never hang a white man for killing Aborigines (see narration eight). Find out what a juror is.
- How do you think this juror's attitude towards Aboriginal people affected his judgement in the trial?
- What safeguards are taken today in trials to prevent people with extreme attitudes from becoming jurors? Is it always effective? Do you know any examples of cases where a juror was discovered to be hostile or in some way seriously prejudiced? Consider the Rodney King case in the USA. Can justice always be assured under the jury system? What are the arguments for and against such a system? Are there alternatives? What are the arguments for and against them?

3 Of the eleven arrested for the Myall Creek massacre only seven were eventually hanged. Were these seven men the only ones responsible for the massacre? Why do you think the Government let the others off?

Capital punishment

1 The characters in the play do not morally question or object to capital punishment as a punishment for crime. Why do you think this is so? What does this tell us about the times in which the play is set?

2 Some people say that capital punishment is 'legalised murder'. What is meant by this expression? How do you feel about capital punishment? Do you agree or disagree with it? Give your reasons.

3 Did the seven men deserve to die for their crime? In which ways did the Government and the landowners 'play politics' with these men's lives? Why do you think they did this? Were their actions justified? Give reasons for your opinions.

4 How is capital punishment supposed to deter crime? Is it effective in doing this? Does Australia have capital punishment as a punishment for crime today? Which countries today use capital punishment as a means of deterring crime?

5 Activities:
- Collect any newspaper reports concerning capital punishment. How are these reports written? Are they for or against capital punishment? What are the opinions expressed?
- Hold a debate about the hanging of the Myall Creek murderers. Read 'The Ballad of Reading Gaol', Oscar Wilde's poem about the last days of a young man who is about to be executed for his crime. Find other accounts of people sentenced to death (in stories, novels, plays or films).

6 Research:
- Find out how many crimes were punishable by death at the time of the Myall Creek hangings.
- Who was the last person to be executed in Australia for a crime? How long ago did this happen? What was the crime? What was the public reaction to the hanging? How similar or different was this reaction to the Myall Creek hangings? See if you can find any newspaper reports to support your views.

Courage and personal responsibility

1 Two related issues raised by the play are the questions of courage and personal responsibility. What do we usually mean by courage? What examples of courage are there in the play?

2 What does personal responsibility mean? In the play (and in reality) Kilmeister took part in the massacre, but Anderson did not. Hobbs brought the massacre to light, against the wishes of many. Later both Anderson and Hobbs gave evidence against the perpetrators of the massacre, much to the displeasure of many members of the community. What do you think of their actions? What were the risks they ran in taking such actions? How are they examples of people who showed personal responsibility and courage?

English — Language workshop

The questions in this section can be used to explore some of the language issues raised by the play. This could take the form of a written response or a discussion. Questions can be approached individually or in groups.

1 Some words used to describe Aboriginal people in the past are today considered derogatory. 'Gin' is one such word. What does this word mean? In the play it is used to reflect accurately the language and attitudes of the times. Which character uses the word? Who does it refer to in the play? What is his attitude towards its subject? Which character counters his view? How? What is the origin of this word in English? Why do you think it is unacceptable today?

2 At the time of the Myall Creek massacre Aboriginal people were often referred to by the Europeans as 'tame' or 'wild'. What did they mean by this? At the time white people, through their newspapers and in their everyday speech, also referred to Aboriginal people by using other animal analogies or descriptions. What racist attitude did they convey by these descriptions? Which characters in the play use such expressions?

3 It is interesting to note that the kind of racist language used against Aboriginal people was also used against other colonised peoples. Indian, African and Irish people, for example, had often been described in similar racist terms by their British colonisers. What does the use of such racist language suggest to us about the nature of the colonisation process?

4 It is sometimes said that words have power. Often in history words have been used by politicians and others as a way of achieving political ends. Can you find examples in the play of language used in this way.
- What are Scott's political objectives in scene six? How does he use racist and emotive language to try and achieve them? How does Governor Gipps counter his arguments?

- Give examples of racist language used against both Aboriginal and non-Aboriginal people today. What is the purpose or motivation behind this language? Be specific in each case.

5 Research other examples from history of racist language used for political ends. Consider, for example, the use of racist language towards Jews in Germany before and during the Second World War.

6 In scene six Scott demands greater protection for the colonists. Here is his exchange with Governor Gipps.

SCOTT: Your Excellency, we can't afford to be soft with these savages! In the past, force has been the only effective way of stopping their aggressions.

GIPPS: Yes, with the result that for the handful of whites killed by blacks in your district, hundreds of Aborigines have been slaughtered.

SCOTT: Which simply proves my point — we are outnumbered.

GIPPS: You're not serious?

SCOTT: We are few, they are many. That is the simple fact of the matter.

- In the above exchange Scott suggests that white people are the victims of Aboriginal aggression. Where such conflict happened, what were possible reasons for it? (Refer to scene six.) Were the Aboriginal people at Myall Creek a threat to the Europeans there? (See scene five.)
- How does Scott twist Gipps' argument in the above exchange? What is the irony in Scott's response?

STUDY UNITS

- Scott refers to Aboriginal people as 'savages'. What does this word mean? In view of the nature and ferocity of the massacre at Myall Creek, who were the savages?

7 The language used by a character often reveals something of the personality of the character who is speaking. Sometimes, for example, characters will attribute to others negative aspects which they, themselves, possess but do not recognise in themselves. In psychology this is known as 'projection'.
- In scene one, Kilmeister shows himself to be both fascinated and fearful of the Aboriginal known as Daddy. He describes Daddy as a 'cunning devil'. What does he mean by this? In which ways does Kilmeister consider Daddy 'cunning'? In which ways does Kilmeister show himself to be 'cunning'?
- Why does Kilmeister use the word 'devil'? The word devil suggests evil, or wrong-doing. Is there any evidence in the play to suggest Daddy has done anything evil? Is there any evidence in the play to suggest that Kilmeister has committed actions that might be considered evil?
- Dangar, too, attributes negative characteristics to Aboriginal people, whom he describes as 'deceptive and treacherous' (see scene five). Is there any evidence in the play to suggest this is so? How does Hobbs defend the Aboriginal people at Myall Creek against Dangar's accusation? How in the play does Dangar reveal himself to be deceptive and treacherous?

8 In scene four, Plunkett reveals his sensitivity towards his religion when questioned about it by Governor Gipps.

GIPPS:	These are noble sentiments. You are a religious man?
PLUNKETT:	I am a Christian. As is Your Excellency.
GIPPS:	A Catholic?
PLUNKETT:	Yes, sir. A Catholic is a Christian.

What does Plunkett mean by his statement that 'a Catholic is a Christian'? How does this statement reflect the religious conflict occurring in the colony at the time?

9 Spoken language was more formal in the era in which the play is set than it is today. Give examples from the play that illustrate this formality. When does it mostly occur? Which scenes do not have this formality? Why? What does this formality in language tell us about the nature of the society at that time?

10 Read Hobbs' testimony in the trial scene (scene seven) in which he describes the massacred Aborigines. How does Hobbs' speech reflect the courtroom situation he is in? Does Hobbs give us any idea about the feelings he experienced at the massacre site? Which words in his dialogue convey some of his feelings about the massacre?

11 Group the following words or terms from the play under these four headings (some may go into more than one group):
- historical words
- legal words
- common words
- unusual words.

assigned servant, Attorney-General, atrocities, authority, carcasses, convict, conscientious, cowardice, dismemberment, duty, executed, expire, eye-witness, Governor, government service, grievances, impunity, intimidated, massacre, magistrate, marauding, mawkish, muskets, mutilated, Negro, landowner, overseer, perjure, perpetrators, property, provocation, prudent, run, slaughtered, squatter, station, stench, stockman, surveyor of lands, tame, testify, ticket-of-leave, treacherous, trial, unscrupulous, verdict.

English and Drama — Literary and performance considerations

This section includes questions for either written or spoken discussion in small groups or individually. There are also creative writing opportunities and improvisational activities.

Characterisation

1 How is the character of Kilmeister portrayed in the play? (Refer to scenes one and two.) In many ways Kilmeister seems to be driven by fears.

- What are some of his fears? Why does Kilmeister react so strongly to Anderson's suggestion that Kilmeister is going mad? What are the strange premonitions Kilmeister has and how do they relate to the events that follow?
- What was Kilmeister's attitude to the Aborigines at Myall Creek? What reason did Kilmeister give for taking part in the massacre? What kinds of pressure, if any, were on Kilmeister to take part? Why do you think he took part?

2 What kind of character is Anderson? What was the name of the Aboriginal woman with whom he was having a relationship? Were such relationships common? Why do you think he did not take part in the massacre? (Refer to scenes one and two.)

3 How is Hobbs' character presented in the play? Why do you think he decided to expose the massacre? (See scenes three and five.)

4 What is Henry Dangar's character like? What is Dangar's attitude to Aboriginal people? Do you think his attitude was typical of many landowners at the time? Dangar told the Police Magistrate at Muswellbrook that Hobbs was of good character, but later dismissed Hobbs from his position without any apparent reason. Why do you think he did this? Consider Dangar's testimony in the trial scene regarding Kilmeister, Anderson and Hobbs. What is ironic about it, given the events shown in the play? Support your answer with reference to the play. (Refer to scenes five and seven.)

5 What kind of character is Plunkett? What is his relationship with the Governor like? Why is he sensitive about his religion? What does this tell us about the society at the time? What is Plunkett's attitude to the squatters? Why does he feel this way? What does he want the Governor to do about the squatters? Why does he see the punishment of those responsible for the massacre as important? (See scene four.)

6 How is Scott portrayed in the play? What organisation does he represent as chairman? What is the purpose of this organisation? Why is he supporting the men accused of the massacre? What is extraordinary about his visiting these men in gaol and what is remarkable about the advice he gave them? What does he demand Governor Gipps do? Does he believe that Aboriginal people have any right to the land? What is his general attitude to Aboriginal people? (See narration six and scene six.)

7 What kind of character is Governor Gipps? What was the state of the colony when he arrived? Why was Gipps' authority in the colony so precarious? Why do Plunkett and Scott irritate him? How does he handle each of these characters? (Refer to scenes four and six.)

8 How does the characterisation work in the play? Do the characters simply represent historical people, or are they used for other purposes? How do the characters reflect the social attitudes of the time? How are the characters used to advance the story and explore the themes of the play? What are the themes of the play?

9 The Aboriginal man called Daddy is one of the off-stage characters in the play. What is meant by this term 'off-stage character'? What was exceptional about Daddy's physical stature?
- In scene one Kilmeister says of Daddy that he 'cured a woman just by singing to her'. What did he mean by this?
- Daddy was a healer, or medicine man, to his tribe. Such people were also referred to as 'clever men' or shamans. Research the

role of these people. What were some of the extraordinary powers they were believed to possess?

10 What other off-stage characters are in the play? How do they contribute to the drama?

Style and performance

1 What is the style of the play? Is the play trying to re-create the historical period exactly? Do the characters speak exactly as they would have in those times? In which ways is it nesssary to modify the language to make it more readily comprehensible for a modern audience? Do all the characters speak in the same style? How are differences in class and education shown in the choice of language for each of the different characters?

2 How is the story told? Why does the play begin just before the massacre? How does the first narration and scene one help us to understand the events that follow? What important off-stage characters are introduced in scene one?

3 How are the scenes linked? What kinds of information are conveyed by the narration passages between scenes? How is this type of narration economical? How does it help the scenes that follow? How do the narration scenes facilitate the flow of the action in a practical way?

4 Costume changes and set changes are minimal, designed to suggest character and location rather than re-create them. What freedom does this approach give the actors in performance? What demand does this approach place on the audience?

5 Describe the pace of the play. Do you think it moves quickly or slowly? How does the pace help the story-telling?

6 Conflict is an important ingredient in drama. What are some of the main conflicts in the play — between characters and between ideas and beliefs?

7 Except for the end of the first trial and the final verdict of the second, the actual trials of the Myall Creek murderers were fairly uneventful from a dramatic point of view, consisting largely of testimonies with little of the tense cross-examinations associated with popular courtroom dramas today. How then is the first trial presented in the play? How is the evidence of the characters in the trial scene important to the purposes of the drama as a whole? How is this scene structured so that it can be achieved by two actors? Refer to narration eight. Why, from a dramatic point of view, is it unnecessary to present the second trial?

Improvisations

1 Imagine Daddy, Ipeta and Charlie as ghostly 'witnesses' at the trial. What evidence would they give? Write the description of what happened at Myall Creek from each of their points of view, and then improvise a scene taking place in the courtroom.

2 Imagine you are one of the the seven prisoners on the night before your execution for your involvement in the massacre at Myall Creek. What are your feelings? Improvise a scene to describe your emotions and reactions.

3 Divide into groups representing different points of view concerning the Myall Creek massacre: Aboriginal people, convicts, squatters and government. Write your feelings about both the massacre and the hangings from each perspective. Improvise scenes between these conflicting groups.

4 Devise a scene to illustrate the notion of personal responsibility and courage based on the following idea. You are with a group of friends and someone suggests that you all do something that you personally disagree with (for example, shoplifting, stealing a car, persecuting somebody because of their race or because they are in some way different). Most want to do it. Some don't. What will you do? How do you handle this situation? How do the others handle the situation?

STUDY UNITS

Convict saves child. Illustration by Charles Nuttall in C. H. Chomley, *Tales of Old Times, Early Australian Incident and Adventure*, W. J. Pater & Co., Melbourne, 1903 (Dixson Library, State Library of New South Wales) This illustration shows an Aboriginal child being sheltered by one of the play's characters. Does the play describe this event? Who would be the most likely character? Did this event take place? If not, why was this drawn?

History and Aboriginal Studies

These questions cover many of the historical, social and political issues raised by the play. They can be used as topics for discussion or debate, or for essays. Many of the questions refer directly to information contained in the play while some require reference to other sources. Students may work individually through the questions, or in groups on selected questions.

1 When the British first came to Australia they declared the country 'terra nullius' — uninhabited or belonging to no-one. Why did they claim this? What consequences did it have for Aboriginal people?

2 One of the great cultural differences between Europeans and Aboriginal people was their differing attitudes to the land. In scene six, for example, Scott states:

> The land belongs to those who make best use of it. The native, through his laziness and unprofitable use of the land, has forfeited that right and deserves to be dispossessed.

What did Scott mean by this statement? What does this statement reveal about the European attitude to land at the time? How did the Aboriginal attitude to land differ? How did Aboriginal people use and manage the land? How did European land practice differ from this? How did these two contrasting uses of land reflect the different lifestyles of the two groups?

3 Who were the squatters? What parts of New South Wales were settled by Europeans in 1838?

4 Was Gipps a popular Governor? What was significant about the orders he had from England regarding Aboriginal people? (See scene four.) What was his relationship like with the wealthy squatters? How powerful were these landowners? Which other governors experienced problems with this group?

STUDY UNITS

5 Henry Dangar and Robert Scott were well-known landowners of the time. Find out more about their lives.

6 How did the spread of European settlement affect Aboriginal people? What happened to Aboriginal people driven from their land? Where did they go? How did they survive? What conflicts occurred because of their displacement?

7 To which nation state did the Aboriginal people at Myall Creek belong? (See narration one.) Name some of its members mentioned in the play. (See scene one.) Had they always lived at Myall Creek? (Refer to scene five.) Why do you think they were at Myall Creek? Why were there mostly women, children and old men at Myall Creek at the time of the massacre? See if you can find out more about this tribe.

8 The Myall Creek massacre was but one of many massacres of Aboriginal people in the north-west of New South Wales. Which other massacres happened around this time in this area? Were these massacres isolated incidents or were there connections between them? Find Myall Creek on a map.
- Draw a map of the area and indicate on it the places where massacres have taken place. Find out about other massacres that have occurred in other parts of Australia. When and where was the last recorded massacre?
- Massacres were but one cause of Aboriginal deaths. What were some other causes of Aboriginal deaths brought about by the process of European colonisation in Australia?

9 Did Aboriginal people resist European colonisation? Give examples of when and where such resistance took place.

10 The Myall Creek massacre was brought to light mainly due to the efforts of the overseer, Hobbs. Many other massacres, however, went undetected and unpunished by the Government. How was this possible? What factors helped to keep such events hidden?

11 What were conditions like for convict stockmen at the time? What were relations like between the two stockmen, Anderson and

61

Kilmeister, and the Aboriginal people at Myall Creek? How did the convicts' experience of life in the bush help form such relationships? Why was it difficult for convicts to escape in the bush? (Refer to scene one in your answers.)

12 Although extraordinary, the hanging of the seven men for the Myall Creek massacre was not the first time a non-Aboriginal had been executed for murdering an Aboriginal person. On what other occasion had this happened? See if you can find out about this incident. Were its circumstances similar or different to the Myall Creek incident? Can you find any other examples of times when white people were punished or threatened with punishment over the murder of Aboriginal people? Why was the punishment of white people for this crime so rare?

13 Certainly, to many people in the colony at the time, the hanging of white men for murdering Aboriginal people was considered outrageous. What do you think the Government was trying to achieve by hanging white men for the Myall Creek murders? Do you think they were successful? It is interesting to note that this was the last time Europeans were hanged for massacring Aboriginal people. Is there any significance in this?

14 One of the men hanged for the Myall Creek massacre was not white. What was his name? (See narration five.) Was there any irony in his participation in the massacre? What further information can you find out about this man?

15 Did the fact that the seven men hanged were convicts and ex-convicts at the time of the massacre have any bearing on their fate? Would it have been as easy for the authorities to hang wealthy squatters? Two days after the execution of the seven men for the Myall Creek massacre the *Sydney Gazette* said:

> Reason and experience alike conspire to impress us with the belief that the unhappy beings who have just suffered, if they did not actually act under the orders of some higher and concealed party, were at least persuaded that in doing as they did

STUDY UNITS

they were acting in accordance with the wishes of their superiors, whom it was both their interest and their desire to please.

Who were the superiors referred to in the quote? Why are they described as the 'concealed party'? Which characters in the play might fit into this group? What point is the article making about their role in the massacre? The article later continued:

If there be any actual ground for the supposition that the unfortunate men who have suffered were urged to the commission of the atrocious deed by parties yet behind the curtain, we trust that no pains will be spared that may lead to the detection of the more than double murderers.

What action is the paper calling for regarding 'parties yet behind the curtain'? Why are they accused of being 'more than double murderers'? To what degree were landowners responsible for the actions of their employees? Were their attitudes towards Aboriginal people contributing factors in the massacres that happened?

16 Originally twelve men were arrested for the massacre. One man, however, managed to escape (see narration five). What was his name and what was significant about him? Despite a reward for his capture, he managed to stay free and live quite openly. Why do you think this man was able to live so openly and avoid arrest?

17 There were many other social problems and conflicts between different groups in the young colony (see narration four). What were some of these social problems? Which other groups opposed each other? In each case, what were the issues that divided them?

18 One conflict touched on in the play is the conflict between Catholic and Protestant. What was the source of this conflict? Why was it such an issue in the colony? Why is Plunkett's position as Attorney-General so significant? Was it easy for Catholics to achieve such positions?

19 Research the newspapers of the day. Which were hostile in their attitudes towards the Aboriginal people and which were not? What were the views they expressed about the massacre and the hangings?

20 Research Gipps' governorship after the massacre. What consequences did the hangings have for Governor Gipps? What were his relations like with the squatters? When did Gipps leave the colony? Was his term as Governor successful in stopping the violence between Aboriginal people and Europeans?

21 How does the treatment of Aboriginal people in Australia during the nineteenth century fit into the larger pattern of colonisation that was occurring in other parts of the world at the time? What were the names of the European colonising powers and what were their colonies? How did other indigenous peoples fare under the control of the various colonial powers?

22 Charles Darwin, during his famous voyage on the *Beagle,* visited the young colony of New South Wales in the mid-1830s, just a few years prior to the massacre at Myall Creek. Darwin's theories about evolution, developed during this voyage and afterwards, were later interpreted by others as scientific support for their racist ideas. In particular, Darwin's ideas of natural selection and the survival of the fittest were seized upon by some to support the already long-established belief in white superiority.

- What did Darwin mean by these ideas? How were they later used by racists? In which ways were they used to justify white superiority and the colonisation process?
  In scene six, which character expresses such views?
  How was the massacre at Myall Creek an example of these attitudes in action?
- Give an example in the twentieth century of the misuse of Darwin's notions for the purposes of racial persecution.

23 Despite all that has happened to Aboriginal people since the arrival of Europeans, Aboriginal culture has survived. Today there is a strong resurgence in Aboriginal identity and values. What is meant by Aboriginal identity and what are some examples of Aboriginal values? How are Aboriginal people maintaining their identity and asserting their values in today's Australian society?

Mounted Police and Blacks. In Colonel Mundy, *Our Antipodes*, 1857 (Mitchell Library, State Library of New South Wales). Violence in the colony between Aboriginal and non-Aboriginal people took many forms. Aboriginal people were not always the victims of massacres; many battles were fought. Study the details of the sketch carefully. How does the incident shown in this drawing differ from the events that happened at Myall Creek?

Suggested reading

The following is a selection of available books and other reading materials useful in researching topics and answering questions set within the study units. Many other books and resources relevant to the topic may be found in your library, or listed within some of the texts below.

Australian Dictionary of Biography, vols 1&2, Melbourne University Press, Carlton, 1966, 1967.

Elkin, A.P., *Aboriginal Men of High Degree*, University of Queensland Press, St Lucia, Queensland, 1977.

Fraser, Bryce, *The Macquarie Book of Events*, Macquarie Library Pty Ltd, St Leonards, Sydney, 1983.

Milliss, R., *Waterloo Creek: A Colonial Cover-up*. McPhee Gribble, Ringwood, Victoria, 1992.

Ramson, W.S., 'The Historical Study of Australian English', *The Macquarie Dictionary*, Macquarie Library Pty Ltd, St Leonards, Sydney, 1981.

Reece, R.H.W., *Aborigines and Colonists,* Sydney University Press, Sydney, 1974.

Rowley, C.D., *The Destruction of Aboriginal Society*, Pelican Books, Ringwood, Victoria, 1972.

Therry, R., *Reminiscences of Thirty Years' Residence in New South Wales and Victoria*, Sydney University Press, Sydney, 1974.

Colonial newspapers: *Sydney Gazette, Sydney Herald, Sydney Monitor, The Australian* and the *Colonist* are available from various libraries, including the Mitchell Library, Sydney.

Official records to do with the Myall Creek massacre, including Supreme Court records and information to do with the trial of the Myall Creek men, can be found at the Archives Office of New South Wales. The Mitchell Library, Sydney, also holds documents of importance about the massacre.

For EU product safety concerns, contact us at Calle de José Abascal, 56–1°, 28003 Madrid, Spain or eugpsr@cambridge.org.

www.ingramcontent.com/pod-product-compliance
Ingram Content Group UK Ltd.
Pitfield, Milton Keynes, MK11 3LW, UK
UKHW041421180426
11947UKWH00007B/231